Your Guide To Becoming The Best Version Of You

Your Guide To Becoming The Best Version Of You

Arissa August

Contents

Contents

Introduction

If you have ever had the desire to become a better you, this book is the push you need to access the potential locked inside of you. First of all, kudos to the ones who do want to become better. We are here to evolve, be better, and awaken. With that being said, there are times when the feeling of stagnation creeps in, leaving you to feel unempowered or confused. That's okay! It is inevitable that feelings of discouragement may come, but it builds your character.

The things you have been through are a direct reflection of just how great you can become. You must do the work to evolve and become the best you and I believe this book is the key you need. As you begin in this book, I want you to understand the odds that you have beat to get here. To be in a mental space to want better for yourself is already a success. Now that you have taken some steps to become a better you, be consistent.

Consistency is the key to your growth. You can have all of the tools needed to become better, and you do, but if you are not consistent how will you succeed? If you get discouraged on this walk of accessing your potential and becoming the best you, remember your why. Why do you want to be better? For many of you, there is a quiet voice inside of you that is so loud at the same time telling you that you were made for more. That voice telling you that you were not created to struggle or be depressed. Grab a hold of that voice and let it be the motivation you need to keep going. There is a reason you desire success. There is a reason you desire to be better. Keep on going.

As you go forth in this book remember that you must apply the knowledge learned and remain consistent. The steps in this book that I provide are proven to work if you truly apply them in your life. They work because the steps are divinely inspired. The Bible truly is the blueprint for peace, happiness, and financial success. In addition to The Bible, there are so many books that are divinely inspired and they are worth adding to your journey of growth. This book allows for much self-reflection, it requires you to be honest with yourself. I can also recommend coming back to certain chapters of this book that may stick out to you more than others. When a chapter resonates more than another, sometimes it means that it is an area you need to focus on a bit more. Allow yourself to immerse in the text and focus on one chapter at a time. This is because each chapter focuses on a key to becoming the best version of yourself. This book holds a key to much inner work that you will have to partake in on your self-growth journey. Because inner work can be heavy, it is important to have a foundation of prayer, ensuring you are asking for the peace and guidance of God as you navigate the road to becoming the best version of yourself. Your inner work journey likely won't stop after completing this book, however, this is a great start. This book should be considered as a key. If followed correctly, you will unlock your potential in different ways. It also holds the key to obtaining new knowledge. You will become hungry for new knowledge, knowledge that will help you be a better you.

I must disclose that not everyone is ready to grow or evolve. With that being said, there may be someone who reads this book who is not yet ready to grow because of how much effort it takes, sometimes it is too much of a heavy task at the time for the individual. That is okay. Those who are not ready should not be deterred from moving forward with reading this book because it can plant a seed that will later sprout into something great. One lesson I can give before we begin chapter one is the importance of timing. As this book plants a seed within you, please remember that your journey is unique to you. Understand that you will sprout when it is your time but you must put in the work. Do not become discouraged when the timing is not what you deem to be the right timing, trust the process and do your part.

Connection With The Source

Connect to The Source; Access Your Purpose

Connecting to The Source is essential for your growth. The Source is The Creator, The Light, and The Voice inside many of us that leads and guides us. Many of us call Him God, or Yahweh. You might question why it is so imperative that you connect to The Source. Well think about it this way; The Source gives light and we need our path to be illuminated so we know where to go. The amount of people who feel lost often points back to the fact that they have not connected to The Source. We must understand that to receive divine instruction and thrive in this world, it is imperative that we connect with The One who created everything.

Do you know what your purpose is? If you answered no, you've got work to do. Surely you don't believe you were put on this earth to not add value in some way. You have to be useful in some way. Think about a potter who creates pottery specifically so he can use it in his home. This potter only creates what is useful and does not waste his materials on creating pottery for fun or boredom, he is intentional with his creations. The potter expects his creations to do what he created them for, otherwise, they become useless and are at that point taking up space. Similarly, God has put amazing gifts in His people and He expects us to do what He asks of us. God expects you to use the gifts He put in you, to be useful in this world. Your gifts and talents are intentional, you were created for a purpose. It is under-standable that not knowing what it is you are called to do may deter you. Ask Yahweh what it is you are called to do on this earth. So many of you have so much value to add to humanity but you have to access it and unlock it to share with the world. Imagine being blessed with so many gifts and talents and not sharing them in any way. Take a moment to think of the people who have poured love and light into you. Where would you be if they had not done that? In the same way, think of the people who are waiting for a beautiful energy like yours to pour love and light into them.

When considering the creation of you, think of all the effort and energy that went into it. I am talking about God choosing you before you were conceived. The traits and gifts that He put into you. Now think of conception, think of your mother carrying you in her womb. This is a quick description but there is so much effort and energy that went into the creation of you. Glory to Yahweh.

Now consider those gifts and talents that God hand-picked and put into you. Like really, consider it. Think about how important you must be. Now would be a great time to take a moment to write down the talents and gifts that God has blessed you with, and tell Him thank you. If you don't know your talents yet, that's okay. That is why you must connect with The Source. I must add that some believe all gifts and talents have to be about singing, playing an instrument, or being a pastor of a church. This is not the case for everyone and your talents are just as important as the ones that get the most attention. Find your purpose and fall in love with using the gifts and talents that Yahweh has blessed you with.

For the ones who know what their talents and gifts are but are choosing not to use them, this is your sign. I am not telling you how to use your talents nor am I giving you a timeline of when you must start. That is between you and The Creator. Again, you must connect with The Source for instruction. What I am saying is that if God has given you something to do then why are you not doing it? Is it fear holding you back? Are you wondering about how the world will perceive you? Is it finances that are keeping you stagnant? Whatever it is, you must know that nothing is too hard for God, so talk to Him about it. But just know, He sees the effort you put in.

Purpose and Parenting

I want to take a moment to applaud the parents. Parents have such a great purpose and it is not to be overlooked. Parents have been entrusted by Yahweh to protect, love, and nurture their children. Sometimes your purpose, or at least one of your purposes, is to pour time, attention, and greatness into your children because their purpose is so great. This does not mean God won't give you other tasks to complete simultaneously, but the task of parenting is a great one. Consider for a moment just how greatly someone's childhood can shape their future. Parents have the ability to add greatness to the world just by being an amazing parent. So if you are a parent reading this book, continue to grow and become the best version of yourself because you're not only helping yourself, but you're also helping the children around you. You can break generational curses just by working on yourself and refusing to introduce toxic beliefs and systems to your children. The goal should be to raise your children in a peaceful and safe environment. If you are someone who did not grow up in an environment of tranquility, providing that for your children is a blessing that will add much value to you and your children. So remember just how important your job is as a parent and strive to be a great one.

How To Connect With The Source

The golden question so many ask is, how to hear God's voice? I cannot tell you how you will hear God's voice, but I can give you some tips on how to start. The first thing I will recommend is understanding who the Creator is. He is The Creator but He is also a Father. It is so important that we understand this. Understanding that God is The Father is something I believe to be a major key in building a bond and a relationship. Why? Because this allows for a more personal connection. When you realize that you should be communicating with Him daily, not just to ask for things, but to simply converse with The Father of creation. Now remember, with God being our Father, you must respect Him. When you are conversing with The Father, remember that He is righteous and we should speak to Him with respect. Next, I would like to recommend praying. If you want to hear from God, simply ask Him. But here is the key, when you ask Him to show Himself to you, you must trust that He will. A relationship with God thrives best when faith is present. In addition to praying, reading The Bible is imperative. The Bible is something that gives us access to the way God speaks and thinks. Now, we have to understand that there will be some mystery to God because He is so great, that our minds cannot understand Him to the full extent, however, the Bible gives a great depiction of His love. From the love story of Yahweh's grace amongst His children to the teachings of Yahshua, the Son of God.

{ **2** }

Commencement

Make A List, A Winner's List

In order to grow into the best version of you, you must first identify what it is that you want. What is it that you want out of life? Do you want health? Do you want to live a life of serving others and spreading joy? Do you want to start a business? Truly take some time to identify what it is you want. Write your goals and reflect on how you will remain true to yourself to access your goals. When you write your goals, it allows you to not only materialize them but you are now holding yourself more accountable being that they are on paper. Writing your goals also allows you to get more specific about what it is you truly desire. So, instead of just thinking in your mind what you want to achieve, write down what it is that you will achieve. If you get tired or dis-couraged you can go back to that piece of paper with your list of goals to remind yourself just how important the goals are to you.

High Vibrational Foods

How are your eating habits? Now I am fully aware that we live in a world that deliberately puts out toxic food for the population to consume. With that being said, we still have a choice. Although many do not grow their own produce, we can still opt for healthier choices in the stores. Why is it so important to eat healthy? For one, healthy food gives energy. Real energy. Your body will love you for taking care of it. It starts by making small changes. Like ensuring you're drinking water, adding whole foods to your diet, refraining from foods filled with chemicals, and not eating pork. Before you try and justify why pork is an acceptable food let's analyze why we should not eat pork. A pig is an animal that does not sweat. Sweating is important for detoxification. In addition to that, pigs eat scraps and are considered dirty animals when it comes to the consumption of the proteins you choose to eat. If you don't think the diet of an animal is important, consider why grass-fed beef is healthier and generally tastes better, and consider why the milk of grass-fed cows has more nutrients. These are proven and have been backed by science. Now let's consider the Bible. Yahweh told His children that the pig, amongst many other animals, was unclean. What are the odds that thousands of years later science has proved this to be true? Now, of course, those who decide to eat certain foods are not to be judged, the Bible is clear on this. However, whether you follow certain laws or not, the food you eat matters. God cares about the foods we put into our bodies. Why? Because our bodies are a temple so we must love and honor them by consuming nutritious foods. Many go by the 80/20 rule when choosing what to consume. You have to be realistic with yourself when making healthy changes regarding diet and exercise. The 80/20 rule encourages one to consume healthy and whole foods 80 percent of the time, while the other 20 percent allows for things people consider comfort foods or treats. Once you begin to implement a healthier diet into your lifestyle, you may notice clearer thinking and more energy. Love your body and be mindful of what you eat, your body will in return love you more for it.

Work it Out

In addition to putting healthy foods into your diet, how are your exercise habits? Do you take time to get outside for a nice stroll? Do you go to the gym? Do you partake in at-home workouts? I can understand that being busy with a typical job can make it harder to exercise, however, you have to find a way. Sometimes the cure for anxiety and depression is a consistent workout schedule. Science proves how important it is for our minds and bodies to exercise. Please keep in mind I am not a nutritionist or a doctor so, consult with one if need be. However, making these changes can be the commencement of your glow-up, becoming the best you. Your workout plan should be specific to you. Do not be deterred by the bodybuilders who portray a standard that may not be realistic for you. The goal is to be healthy, and for you, that could mean a very simple workout. Some individuals benefit more from a less intense workout. If you are unsure about the workout plan for you, do some research and get to know your body and what works for you. Again, the goal is to be healthy.

Self Care Days

Designated days for self-care are so important in becoming the best version of you. These types of days can include things like spending time in nature, journaling, or going to a nice spa. These self-care days do not have to include spending large amounts of money, but they do have to include doing something that genuinely brings peace and tranquility. I want to emphasize just how beneficial it is to spend time in nature. The trees, the grass, and the ocean are all great ways to induce relaxation. Yet another reason to thank God for His creations, He is so very intentional. The simple act of spending time amongst the trees has been scientifically proven to lower anxiety and stress.

{ **3** }

Your Inner Child

Reparenting Your Inner Child

For some, your inner child is crying. Crying because they did not receive the love and validation they needed to thrive. This will show up in adulthood if not dealt with. This is why there are people who are filled with anger, this is why so many struggle with anxiety and depression. It stems from childhood. I am not a psychologist, however, this is a known fact. A person's childhood often shapes their future. If you are someone who grew up in struggle or endured abuse, you don't have to allow it to dictate your life any longer. We are often taught to avoid living in the past and to let things go, this is true. However, when it comes to things like childhood trauma, sometimes it requires a bit more work. It is easy for someone to tell you to just let it go but we must remember that most of our traits whether good or bad are a product of the environment we grew up in. Do not let anyone

{ 12 }

invalidate your experiences as a child, if it bothers you then take the necessary steps to overcome whatever it is that you endured so you can release it. Reparenting your inner child is a very important part of your journey to becoming the best version of yourself. Researchers have studied and found many correlations between a toxic childhood and toxic adult relationships. Sometimes, in order to start attracting those great things you desire, you have to heal your inner child. You have to look at emotional trauma like a blockage. When someone has an energetic blockage, they can energetically repel the good things that are meant for them. This is not to say that what is for you will not find you, however, if you are not ready for what is for you then how will you properly handle it? Understand that God allowed you to go through some things in childhood but His intention for humanity was only peace, love, and harmony. His intention was not for humanity to suffer but we must remember that people do in fact have free will. With that being said, your childhood trauma does not mean that you are not loved by God. Your childhood trauma is a reflection of the fact that you are resilient and even protected. As you work on removing the blockages, remember just how good God is and ask for His guidance and assistance in your growth.

Forgive Your Caregivers

Start with forgiving your caregivers. Some did the best they could with what they had and some just did not know any better. Even if you had a caregiver who deliberately caused trauma, you must forgive them. I cannot tell you exactly why they did what they did or did not do what they needed to do, but what I can tell you is this; a very major key in your success is healing your inner child. Caress your inner child, validate your inner child. It is needed. If you want to stop attracting toxic situations or even just experience more peace, healing your inner child may be the next step for you. Anxiety and depression are both symptoms of a toxic childhood. Forgiving your caregivers requires compassion and understanding. It is very likely that your caregivers also experienced childhood trauma that you may not even be aware of. This also goes for the caregiver who deliberately inflicted abuse or trauma. They also likely had things they were dealing with. Understand that forgiving them does not excuse what they did but forgiveness is the key to your peace.

How To Reparent Your Inner Child

There are so many ways to reparent your inner child, but I suggest starting with prayer. I won't tell you what to say to Him but spend some time meditating and speaking with God about this. Yahweh was there during your childhood and knows things you may not even remember about your childhood. Another thing I highly recommend is saying positive affirmations. Affirmations are something we will cover in-depth in a later chapter, a very important part of your journey to becoming the best version of yourself. Some great inner child affirmations are, "I am safe", "I am protected", and "My inner child is worthy of a fulfilling and happy life". These are a few affirmations you can say, but I highly recommend doing some research to find what affirmations best suit you. Doing research on reparenting your inner child can be the start of something amazing. For some, counseling may be the best option. Find out what is best for your specific situation and put the work in.

Talk to Your Inner Child

Imagine yourself as a child. Maybe even pull up a photo of you as a child. Tell her/him that she/he is valuable. Tell them they are loved and understood and they are now safe. Now hug yourself. I know, it sounds odd but sometimes the little version of you just needed a hug, a real hug from someone who really loved you. Now, you have the opportunity to be the positive and loving person you needed growing up for yourself. When you make decisions about your growth and self-care, remember that your inner child is still inside of you. That younger version of you is counting on you to be successful and to make good choices daily.

{ **4** }

Deal With Anger

Emotions Are Energy

You must deal with anger. Anger can literally cause sickness in the body if not properly dealt with. Anger is a powerful emotion and can be very dangerous when it is not channeled correctly. You have to think of anger or any emotion as energy. If you hold all of that negative energy inside and don't release it, what do you think will happen? There are healthy ways to process the emotion of anger.

It is important to understand that some have anger that they are holding onto from years prior. Anger as well as fear or stress can manifest itself into sickness if not dealt with properly. The body releases stress chemicals as a result of anger and it does trigger a bodily response called fight or flight. Fight or flight is a natural response for humans that is designed to protect us from harm's way. This is because humans had to survive in the wilderness at some point in evolution and the fight or flight response kept us safe. Although we have evolved as humans, our bodies will remain protective of us. Studies have been done to show that when someone gets angry, their body releases adrenaline and cortisol. These are stress hormones that cause a reaction in the human body. This is not a bad thing, because again, our bodies are designed to protect us. But oftentimes when someone makes us angry, there is no real physical threat. This is not to say your emotion of anger is invalid, I am simply showing you just how powerful the emotion of anger can be. You must deal with anger and release the toxic energy you may be holding inside.

As you know, the mind and the body cannot be separated. This statement is a fact and should be deeply analyzed. Part of caring for your body is ensuring you are caring for your mind. There is a high correlation between stress and disease. I emphasize this because it needs to be deeply understood. I want you to understand how toxic it is for your body when you internalize emotions like anger. Many scientific studies have shown that anger suppresses the immune system. The immune system is complex and made up of cells, tissues, and organs. The immune system fights off disease, bacteria, and sickness, and is very important in protecting the body. Now that you know anger suppresses the immune system, you should understand how serious it is to manage and release these emotions. You must protect your body, it is your job. You have to make it a priority to manage your anger and stress.

How To Deal With Anger

First I want you to identify what it is you are angry about. This may take some time as it could be something you're holding on to from years prior. Is it because someone is mistreating you? Are you holding onto trauma from your past? Is it your situation? Are you struggling mentally or financially? Now ask yourself if there is something you can do about this. If it is something regarding trauma from the past, you may need to focus on inner work and forgiveness to overcome it. There are times when there is something you can do about it but sometimes God wants you to push through, diamonds are formed under pressure. Now when I say God may want you to push through, I am not implying to internalize your anger. You must still release these emotions. To push through means to understand where you are and continue to persevere and trust the process. When dealing with this emotion called anger, you are not going to use violence or speak unkind words to the person that may be causing the emotions. You are not going to speak unkind words to yourself. This will just perpetuate the cycle and the emotion will still be undealt with. Channel this energy to do something good.

A great thing to do is pray. Pray because the Spirit of God can bring peace that no one else can. After you pray, a great thing to do may be to exercise. Working out and sweating is a great way to release toxins from the body as well as unprocessed emotions. Another way is to connect with nature through grounding. This is a technique that is not talked about enough but it does work. Grounding is when you stand barefoot in soil or grass and allow the soil to absorb the negative energy from your body. Many who are carnal-minded will not understand the power of this technique and that is okay but you who are reading this book, give it a try. You have to understand how intentional God was when He created the world. The plants, the ocean, and the soil are all multi-purpose. If you need more proof, studies have also been done to suggest that grounding does improve the mood. There are plenty of positive and healthy ways to deal with anger. It is important that you not only deal with it but deal with it correctly.

Scientific Study on Holding in Anger

There have been many scientific studies on anger and how it affects health. Realistically, many repressed emotions such as anxiety, depression, or worry can cause health issues. With this knowledge, we must do better. We must take care of ourselves mentally, spiritually, physically and emotionally. You have to love yourself and refuse to allow anger to control you or your health. One way to keep anger from causing sickness is to not get angry in the first place. For example, if someone makes you angry, you do not have to respond. Keep in mind that choosing not to respond does not mean repressing the emotion you may feel, I am not implying that you internalize the anger by not responding. I am simply saying that if someone can control your emotions, they can control you. Once you do the inner work required for growth, certain things will no longer anger you. Grab hold of the peace of God so tightly that the ignorant actions of others rarely affect you. Now remember, you are human and emotions are natural so there may be times when something does bother you. With that being said, do not try and pretend something doesn't affect you by repressing emotions because that is not strength, strength is when you deal with your emotions. Remember, when you repress your anger it can lead to sickness. So if you do feel an emotion surfacing, deal with it properly.

Don't Stress

There will be times when stress comes and you have to learn how to deal with it. It would be silly to expect to never feel worried or stressed about something. Even the smallest task can make someone stressed and that is because you are human! The key to overcoming stress is knowing how to release the emotion and feeling. God will sometimes allow people to be in a season of stress because they have something they need to learn. The stress you endure is not always about breaking you down. Instead, it's about growing you. For example, you could be stressed about how you will pay a bill or a new job you are waiting for. During that time of waiting and wondering, God is expecting you to have faith. Now with faith must come work, as told in the Bible, however, if you're working but God is still making you wait, you must trust His timing and have faith. A very important thing to remember is that during this time of waiting, you must find a hobby or an exercise that allows you to release the emotion of stress. Much like anger, stress can cause sickness as well. The reason why stress causes sickness is because many do not release the emotion, they either complain about it or pretend they are not stressed. This is not what you should do. Yes, express how you feel to God and pray, but complaining is not how to do it. Also, do not give silent treatment and pretend that nothing is wrong. Some ways to release stress include taking a shower, walking in nature, crying to release the emotion, praying, and writing out or thinking about the things you are grateful for. There are many ways to release the stress you may be dealing with so find what works best for you and begin to practice it when needed.

Stop The Gossip

Gossiping Will Drain Your Energy

When you choose to stop gossiping or partaking in conversations of gossip, a level-up happens. Gossiping is low vibrational activity and requires energy that could be used to do something better for yourself. I believe choosing not to gossip is a great way to become a better you. Many were raised in a home where gossiping was considered normal and acceptable. It is not. God is against gossip and gossiping does not positively add to your growth. We talked about emotions being energy and in the same way, gossiping and speaking out negativity about others feeds bad energy. The goal is to repel bad energy, not feed it. Become so confident in yourself that gossiping no longer interests you. This may take some work but God notices effort.

High Vibrational

High-vibrational individuals do not want to partake in conversations of gossip. When you begin to elevate and become the best version of yourself, you will likely feel drained by gossiping, it will no longer interest you. Why? Because you are vibrating at a higher and more positive frequency. If you analyze why people gossip, it sometimes stems from the fact that they are not very happy with themselves. Don't let that be you. If you are unhappy with your life, gossiping is not going to make you a better person. You are only lowering your frequency by partaking in gossiping. You must do the work if you want to be the best version of yourself.

Inner Circle

Your inner circle and friendships cannot thrive off of gossip. You must find something more conducive and positive to talk about. If you find yourself around people who do not respect your desire to refrain from gossip, it may be time to get a little bit of distance. This does not mean being rude or disrespectful but it means protecting your peace and being mindful of the company you keep. It is so important to be around people who are also striving to become the best version of themselves in some way. The goal is to feel energized after hanging around your inner circle. You have to get to the point where negativity is no longer entertaining to you. You have to be so involved in becoming the best version of yourself that gossiping becomes an activity you are repelled by. With this knowledge, we must know that being repelled by certain activities does not mean you become arrogant. It simply means you love yourself and others enough to set a positive example.

It is important to understand that as you work on becoming the best version of yourself, your inner circle may change. During this time of raising your vibration, you will most likely no longer be in alignment with the people you once befriended. This is because you are no longer a vibrational match and that is okay. As you become the best version of yourself, you will repel people and situations that are not for you. You will repel situations that are considered low vibrational. Friends you once spent much time with will no longer care to hang around you and you will no longer care to hang around them. This is especially true when telling your friends you no longer want to partake in gossip. Your real friends will respect this decision but some may take offense to it. If there are people around you who do not respect your desire to grow and become better, do not let that stop you from wanting to be better. Continue on your path of self-reflection and growth.

Give Grace

As I mentioned, many were raised around gossip so it has been normalized. Sometimes people are genuinely not aware of just how toxic it is to gossip so it is important to be understanding of this. People have developed a habit of gossiping and it is not something they deem unacceptable. As you begin to work on yourself and refrain from gossip, you have to give yourself grace and give others grace when trying to overcome bad habits that are being partaken in. This means understanding and showing compassion to the people around you. Your efforts won't always be met with agreement but God knows your heart. These things can take time but if you want to become the best version of yourself, you must start.

Focus On You

The majority of people thrive off of focusing on other people's drama. This is commonly accepted in society. From people posting their drama on social media to reality shows that promote drama as their main theme. What will set you apart from most people is not focusing on drama. It may seem fun or interesting but it truly does not benefit you. If you find yourself sticking your nose in other people's drama, craving updates on their mess, you have work to do. You have to realize that what you put your energy toward matters. If you want to become better why would you entertain drama? The Bible warns that we should not rejoice in others' downfalls. Making it a priority to get updates on drama feeds toxicity. It is understandable and very normal to be interested in drama, but that does not make it right. The human mind may find interest in drama for different reasons. One reason is that it can serve as mental stimulation. Another reason is that focusing on the drama of others can serve as a distraction from the things people may be dealing with. Although there are scientific justifications as to why many crave and entertain drama, that does not make it right. The reason I explain the science behind it is so that you can find a way out based on your specific situation. For example, if you find yourself entertaining drama frequently, it may be because you lack purpose. This is not to say that people in their purpose do not entertain drama, but overall, when you are focused on your purpose, you have less time for drama. Another reason is that many were raised in a home where their bonding time may have consisted of entertaining drama and talking about drama amongst each other. Get to the bottom of why you may entertain drama frequently and make a choice to focus on more positive things.

{ 6 }

Self-Concept

The Way You Think Of You

It would be silly to expect the best treatment from others while treating yourself disrespectfully. You should think of yourself highly in the sense that you deserve the best things and the best relationships. When I say think of yourself highly, I am not endorsing arrogance, you should never be arrogant. What I am saying is that you should think of yourself as someone who holds high standards and demands respect. This includes self-talk. How do you speak to yourself? Is it with kindness? Is it with patience and respect? Many people will use negative self-talk and not realize the power behind their words. Those same people will become upset if someone speaks to them as negatively as they talk to themselves. If you want others to speak kindly to you then you must speak kindly to yourself. This does not mean there won't be individuals who speak with disrespect towards you, however, when you speak so lovingly toward yourself you will not tolerate negative talk from others, and you will know your worth. Others will hold you in a higher regard when you hold yourself in a higher regard. You have to treat yourself the way you want others to treat you. Be kind and speak positive words to yourself. Make it a habit to speak daily affirmations that remind you just how important and loved you are. As you may have heard, what you whisper to yourself in silence, others will repeat to you in public. This means that your behavior toward yourself when no one else is there will impact the way people treat you overall. Pay attention to the way people treat you. Most of the time, it is a reflection of how you treat yourself. You have to embody confidence and think and speak highly of yourself.

Self Concept Is The Key

Everything we've discussed in this book so far is meant to guide you to become the best version of yourself, to build your self-concept. Self-concept is a term that describes how you identify yourself. When you raise your self-concept, it will be the motivator you need to continue becoming the best version of yourself. This is because when you see your-self a certain way, you will not want to engage in behaviors that don't align with who you are as a person, or rather who you are becoming as a person. Self-concept is a very important key to becoming who you want to be in your per-sonal and professional life. In other words, you get to decide who you want to be, raising your self-concept allows you to do this. Do you want to be someone who wakes up early every day and does a workout? Do you want to be someone who reads The Bible consistently? Or maybe someone who follows healthy eating habits? Do you want to be someone who owns a successful business? How about someone who embodies true confidence and happiness? You get to decide! Show up as the person you are working to become, even before you reach the goal. This shows faith and it raises your self-concept.

The way you raise your self-concept is by setting a clear goal for yourself. Decide who it is that you want to be and work to become her/him. Once you decide who it is you want to be, you should then behave as though you're already that person. Your daily actions should align with who it is you want to become. You're not going to start acting like her/him tomorrow, it starts today. How does the new version of you dress? How do they talk? How are they in relationships? Whoever you want to become starts now. It doesn't start when you get the money or after you get the dream body. It starts now because you raise your self-concept. As we discuss self-concept it is important that you give yourself grace. You are where you are right now for a reason and it wouldn't be wise to degrade the current version of you to get to the new version of you. You must love yourself and be kind to yourself. Remember, the way you treat yourself is the way others will treat you. Self-concept truly is a form of self-love. Why? Because you're saying that you want better for yourself, you're choosing to create the life you deserve. That's self-love. Again, you cannot raise your self-concept without self-love and acceptance of yourself. I must emphasize just how important it is to truly love yourself during this journey of becoming the best version of yourself.

External Validation

You should not be seeking validation from others. You should remember that your validation comes from The Most High God. If He created you, why would you think you can receive true validation from anyone but Him? Many fail to set meaningful boundaries in relationships because they fear they will no longer be validated by others. People and their emotions change frequently meaning that one day they may validate you and the next day they won't. Humans will be humans and it is not wise to expect a human to validate you. Trust in who you are and who God has called you to be. If you ever feel like you need to be validated, here are some steps you can take. First, pray and ask The Most High to guide you. Second, you are going to go within. Who is it that God says you are? Who do you want to be? That is enough to validate you! This is why self-concept is so important. When you prioritize self-concept, you do not crave external validation because you know who you are.

{ 7 }

Daily Affirmations

Positive Affirmations

If you are a child of God, you should already know how much power your words hold. Let's consider the scientific aspect for a minute. Studies have been done to prove that positive affirmations do work at retraining the mind to think and feel positive. I must add, that these studies came after Yahweh had already revealed this to humanity if one needed more proof of The Creator. God is all-knowing and He is real. Your words are so powerful that they have the opportunity to shape your desired reality. If our words are just that powerful, why are you not speaking against anxiety? Why are you not speaking loving words of affirmation to those around you more often? Why are you not telling yourself just how valuable you are? It is not a myth that positive affirmations work. Your words hold power and it is time to realize just how good things can get when you use positive affirmations. Words of affirmation have the power to reprogram the mind. If you spent time around individuals who spoke negatively towards you, especially as a child, your mind did what the mind does and likely soaked in those words. Now, it is up to you to reprogram your mind and tell yourself that you are loved. The great thing about affirmations is that your mind will begin to believe these positive words after some time. Even if you do not believe it yet, keep speaking positively until you do. Having a toxic childhood or experiencing toxic relationships in adulthood does not mean you cannot have peace. You have the power to feel better and think positively. Use the power God has given to bless yourself and even those around you. Speak positive words of affirmation and begin to experience tranquility.

The Variable and The Constant

Let's look at another study, this is one that can be done at home as well. An individual takes three jars of premade rice and labels them. The first jar says, "I love you" and this phrase is to be repeated to the jar of rice for seven days. The second jar is labeled, "I hate you" and the individual is to repeat this to the jar for seven days. The third jar is considered the constant and does not need a label as the individual will not be repeating any words to the jar of rice for seven days. The experiment is to identify how quickly these jars mold based on their different variables, which in this case would be the different words spoken to them. So what was the outcome? You guessed it! The jar that was spoken to with positive words had no mold. The jar that was spoken to negatively had mold, lots of it. Taking it a step further, the jar with no words spoken to it had molded even slower than the jar that had negative words spoken to it. Once again, science proves the existence of God. It proves what God has been telling us this entire time. Watch your words and make it a habit to speak kindly to yourself and others.

Faith and Assumption

You were likely taught just how powerful it is to have faith in the things you want and pray for. Faith is a big part of obtaining the things you desire. Assumption and faith are so important when stating positive affirmations. You must have faith in what you say and you must assume the affirmations you speak are already true. This is important because you are showing The Most High just how strong your faith is. You can absolutely convince your mind of the positive affirmations you state. This is why positive self-talk is so important. We must remember that the words we speak are powerful.

Complaining

When you complain, you are using energy toward something that likely won't help the situation. Complaining can become a habit and you may not even realize when you're spending your energy complaining. It's very low vibrational to complain and most complaints aren't backed by action or a solution. Your words are powerful, and there's energy behind your words. What type of frequency do you think you're putting out when you're sitting up complaining all day? Again, complaining can be habitual and it can in fact take practice to stop complaining. It's important not to mix up complaining and venting. Venting is what is done when you're expressing how you feel about something, this is necessary. Complaining is when you repeat the same thing over with no intention of presenting a solution. People who don't complain all day aren't free of issues, however, they realize the importance of focusing on the positive and speaking positively. Take a moment to think of someone who is constantly complaining about something. How are they? What type of situations do they mostly attract? If you pay close attention, those who habitually complain usually always have something to complain about. This proves how powerful the frequency of words are. The habitual complainer is usually attracting situations that leave them with more to complain about. If they would just speak positively and stop complaining, imagine what good they could attract. Again, I am not saying it is wrong to vent about what you're feeling, however, if you find yourself complaining in most of the conversations you're having then it is time to correct that behavior.

Good Habits

As you may know, we create habits with repetition. For example, the habitual complainer made a habit of complaining and because of it, they began to attract situations that warranted more reasons for them to complain. You can create the habit of speaking positively. Train your mind to think positive thoughts by correcting your mind each time a negative thought comes. One thing about habits is that they can take time to form so you must continue to train your mind daily and not give up when the results are not instant. You can create the habit of saying positive affirmations each time you get up to start your day. Waking up and stating positive affirmations can produce a more peaceful and positive day. You must create positive habits that will overall help on your journey to becoming the best version of yourself. Again, these things can take time but consistency is the key. You must continue to build positive habits that will contribute to your overall success.

{ **8** }

Love Yourself

Self Love Is Not The Absence of Love For Others

The Word of God is clear that arrogance is not of Him. The Bible says that in the last days, people will be lovers of themselves. So please keep that in mind as we go forth in this chapter. Loving yourself does not entail arrogance nor is it the absence of love for others. The Bible is warning about people who are self-absorbed and only care about them-selves, that is not what I am talking about when I signify the importance of self-love. As you grow and evolve the importance of self-love will become more apparent to you, leading you to attract better situations and people in your life. Loving yourself will make you want to love others, and your peace and joy will radiate onto those around you. So remember, as you work on self-love, you will in return also love others.

What Is Self-Love

If you ask the majority of people if they love themselves, they will likely say yes. The question is, do they actually love themselves? Do you love yourself? Believe it or not, it takes strength and inner work to truly love yourself. When you love yourself, you are going to be mindful of the food you put into your body. This is not to say you do not love yourself if you choose not to eat whole foods all day and every day, but when you love yourself you will not want to overeat junk food. You will prefer to eat healthier foods and be mindful of the ingredients in the foods you buy. When you love yourself, you will want to take care of your mental and emotional health. Sometimes that means going to counseling and sometimes that means having people around you that bring out the best in you. When you love yourself, you will want to build your relationship with Yahweh and be in tune with your higher self. When you do the inner work to truly love yourself, it may not be as simple as you think due to the fact that you will have to shed old and limiting beliefs that you learned as a child, however, the reward is great. Those who practice self-love are intentional about the words they speak about themselves. They are mindful of the music they sing because they know the power of words. Those who love themselves set boundaries in their relationships to ensure they are not being mistreated in any way. They prioritize self-care and are not afraid to stand up for themselves.

The Benefit of Self Love

Loving yourself not only benefits you, it actually benefits other people. Remember, self-love is not arrogance. You might be wondering how self-love could possibly benefit other people. Let me explain. When you do the inner work and truly begin to love yourself, you will be happier. True self-love will radiate in your life and positively affect those around you. When you pour love into yourself, you will become so full of positive energy and love that it will naturally pour out onto others. Because you will be pouring out love toward others, it is also very likely that you will receive more love in return. Many do not realize how powerful love is. The Bible tells us that love covers a multitude of sins so let's analyze that verse. Sin is the reason the world is not going the way God intended. His word tells us how disappointed He was in the creation of mankind all because of sin. Let that sink in so you can understand what sin truly is. The world has desensitized sin and many sinful acts have become normalized but The Most High is clear on how He feels about sin. Yes, God has emotions. Despite God's disappointment in the sinful acts of man, He proceeded to pour love into the Earth to counteract the darkness when He sent His Son. If love can cover a multitude of sins, this confirms just how powerful love is. Some would categorize love as an act, some categorize love as an emotion, and some may say that it is energy. However, love is so strong and so powerful that it is an action, an emotion, and energy. Love is one of the highest forms of energy on Earth, more powerful than sin. With this knowledge, it is important to be someone who pours out love. You must genuinely love yourself and love others as well.

9

Guard Your Heart, Guard Yourself

What You Fill Your Mind With

We talked about affirmations and how important they are. Now let us cover the content we watch or the media we entertain. The amount of shows that are out for the world to indulge in shows why people are constantly angry, anxious, or depressed. You have to start asking yourself why negative media gets the most attention. Why is it that the television shows that promote toxicity get so much attention? There are a few reasons as to why this is the reality. For one, people feed off drama because they are refusing to do their own inner work. In addition to that, the companies that push this media are intentionally targeting specific groups. With this knowledge, we must begin to be completely uninterested in toxic media. This is not to take the fun out of your daily routine, this is so you vibrate at a higher frequency. You will notice a difference in your peace and even in the people you attract in your life when you choose not to entertain mediocrity in content or media. One of the great things about doing inner work is that you will no longer crave to entertain negative media. You will literally feel repulsed or even guilty when indulging in this type of content. This is because you have elevated and are no longer in alignment with the low vibrational activities that once fascinated you.

If you can think back to your youth, you may remember that your caregivers did not allow you to watch certain television shows. This was likely because they knew you should not be exposed to toxicity, especially at a young age. Entertaining toxicity and watching television that promotes drama is just as toxic if it were a kid watching it. The question now is why do many think watching toxic shows in adulthood is acceptable? If it is toxic, why do so many want it? Some have in fact researched the link between watching certain reality shows and anxiety. Unfortunately, many are not aware of this and because of it, people will continue to entertain toxic shows. What you must realize is that when you want to become the best version of yourself, there are many things you must choose to stop entertaining. Becoming the best version of yourself is about improving yourself in different areas. To some, becoming the best version of themselves is only about money, and for others, it's just about exercising and having the figure they desire. Understand that it is about so much more. As previously mentioned, we are here to grow and evolve. There is a higher version of you that may require you to do some inner work to get to. It's not always fun or easy because it may require you to reprogram your mind, forcing you out of toxic habits. You have to get rid of old and limiting beliefs that you were once taught. There are many in this world who are comfortable in their limiting beliefs and because of this, they cannot grow. It's important not to make the mistake of hearing new knowledge and putting it off, it could be your way out. Your way out of anxiety, your way out of poverty, and your way out of stress.

Music and Frequency

The music you entertain is just as important. Consider the popular music being pushed out today. Consider the lyrics and the message they are sending through the music. It is so important that you are mindful of what you listen to. Music can affect your mood, there is scientific proof. Have you ever heard a song that sounds so good you get chills? We are energetic beings! Understand that if a simple song can influence your mind and body to get goosebumps and chills, it is powerful. When an artist gets into the booth and sings a song they wrote or a song that was written for them you must understand there is emotion behind these things. Emotions are what? Energy! Understandably, you may feel attached to certain music artists or genres but a very important part of your level-up journey is to not entertain toxic music. What are the lyrics saying? Are the lyrics promoting violence? Are the lyrics degrading women, men, or The Creator? If so, it might be best to find something else to listen to. This is also a part of self-love. If you love yourself you will not feel right entertaining mediocrity. Music is powerful and it has the ability to change the mood. So understand that what music you listen to does matter.

10

Knowledge

Keep On Learning

Humans are constantly evolving. The mind is made to learn and gain new knowledge. Mental health can decline when you are not actively using your skills or gaining new knowledge. Why do you think people struggle so much with identity and even depression after high school and college? There may be many reasons for this, however, one reason is due to the fact that many have stopped learning new skills. This theory is a case-by-case basis and sometimes does not apply to the one who began working in their purpose or career after finishing high school or college. This is not the reality for everyone and that is okay as it is important not to compare your journey to others. Learning new skills does not always mean enrolling in school, sometimes it's just buying a new book, watching educational videos, or picking up a new hobby. If you are someone who has stopped learning, let this be your encouragement to start. Learning new skills can drastically improve your overall self-worth as well as personal fulfillment. So many people are seeking to be fulfilled and don't know where to start and sometimes gaining new knowledge is the way. We have heard many times that the brain is like a muscle and gaining new knowledge is like exercise for the brain. Science tells us that learning does in fact strengthen the brain. This would explain why repetition in learning is important, it is like a workout. By learning new skills you are encouraging the growth of new brain cells.

New Connections

Learning promotes the growth of new brain cells and builds stronger connections between the brain's neurons. Not only are you building connections in the mind, but you are opening the possibility for new connections on your journey. Learning a new skill can open doors for great opportunities, leading to positive relationships as well as career growth. It is so important to continue learning and it is time to remove the limiting belief that learning stops after attending school. Happiness comes from within meaning you must love and take care of yourself; mind, body, and spirit. Do not fear the act of learning a new skill, it can benefit you in more ways than you may understand at the moment.

Allowing yourself to gain new knowledge will set you apart from the people who are choosing complacency despite the fact that they do not feel happiness. Don't let your desire for knowledge stop. After you complete this book, go find another good book to indulge in. Feeding your mind needs to become the new norm for you if you want to be the best version of yourself. With that being said, pray and use discernment about the knowledge you receive or the books you come across. There is so much knowledge out there and not all of it is good. In The Book of Genesis, the story of Adam and Eve taught us that certain knowledge and the desire for certain knowledge should be avoided. The enticement to learn new knowledge that should have been avoided led humanity into sin and confusion. Had Adam and Eve chosen to obey when The Most High instructed that certain knowledge should be avoided, the world could have been different. When growing and learning, you must pray and use discernment. This can keep you from things that are not for you. Trust that God will lead you to the knowledge for you and keep going.

{ 11 }

Forgive and Release

Forgive and Release

You have to forgive those who have hurt you in the past. One thing we must remember is that everyone is dealing with something, things they do not even speak of to others. This is not to excuse their behavior but it is to say that when they mistreated you, it was likely more of a reflection of who they were and what they were dealing with. Regardless of why they did what they did, release the past. Harboring negative emotions like anxiety, fear, resentment, and anger can hurt you more than you realize. It is so important that you release negative emotions. So many people have been hurt or disrespected and they will either pretend they have forgiven the person that hurt them or they openly acknowledge how they do not forgive them. You must understand that your forgiveness must be genuine and it must come from the heart. It might feel like it is impossible to forgive and it may not feel like the other person deserves it, but forgiveness is really for you. Imagine harboring anger against someone and allowing it to affect you daily, meanwhile, they have moved on but you are still holding onto it. The strong emotions you feel toward that person can and will likely be internalized. Emotions are what? Energy! When you do the inner work to grow into becoming the best version of yourself, you will not want to give others power over your emotions. Remember, forgiving them does not mean they did not do what they did, it means you love yourself and others enough to forgive and release.

How To Forgive

I cannot tell you exactly how to overcome the feelings of unforgiveness because your situation is your situation. What that person did to you could've broken parts of you that you did not even realize could be broken. They may have left you traumatized, sentencing you to a place of distrust and heartache. If that is the case for you, give yourself the grace to overcome whatever it is that you may have endured. Love yourself and cater to your needs as this is essential in overcoming trauma. A very key piece of guidance I can offer in learning to forgive is to look at the person from a different perspective. At some point, this person was a child who may have endured toxicity, abuse, or neglect. The trauma they may have experienced as a child or even in adulthood caused them to develop traits that eventually led to your trauma. This is why doing inner work is so very important, it allows for healthier and more positive relationships. The purpose of understanding their past is to allow yourself to develop compassion and understanding toward them. This is a great way to overcome feelings of unforgiveness because you too were once a child who may have experienced trauma.

An additional piece of advice to offer is to consider the times you did things that required forgiveness. Now you may consider your actions to be less harmful, but to the individual you hurt, those actions may have required them to do work to overcome what you did. Now consider the times you sinned against God and the times He not only forgave you but still blessed you. Surely we must know that God has emotions and it saddens Him when we sin, yet He continues to offer grace and forgiveness. We must be forgiving. It is easier said than done but this is very important when working to become the best version of yourself. When we truly observe unforgiveness and why people are struggling to forgive, it is typically translated into someone doing something that hurt you. That hurt can then grow into anger and from anger, it can turn into unforgiveness. So acknowledge that what they did hurt you, and depending on the situation maybe disclose this information to them, but you must release it. Use discernment and pray for guidance regarding your specific situation, this is important. Most people want to attract better relationships and situations into their lives and sometimes the prerequisite to doing so is not only releasing the ones that weren't for you, but releasing what they did to you. To release someone or something is to make the choice to no longer entertain them or the situation. This means you protect your peace by not allowing them to have unlimited access to you. Another way to release a situation is to pray about it. Humans will be humans and nobody is perfect so give grace and compassion to yourself and to others.

Forgiving The One Who Isn't Sorry

Again, we have to understand why people behave the way they do. This is never to excuse their behavior but instead to have the heart of love and compassion that God wants for His people. Forgiving someone who isn't sorry doesn't make you weak, it makes you strong. This does not mean putting yourself in a position to be hurt by them again, but it means you should love yourself enough to move forward. The Bible is clear that we do not wrestle against flesh and blood. This means that because we are spiritual beings in a spiritual world, things we encounter are deeper than the carnal mind may realize. There are energies and spiritual forces that can influence people to act in certain ways. You have people on this earth who have hearts of purity, kindness, and love despite the odds against them. You also have people on this earth who may have gone through so much at a young age and now their pain has been translated into anger, hatred, and the opposite of good. With this information, you can move forward with compassion but also with caution. It is imperative that with new knowledge, you do not judge people through ill intent but to judge with righteous judgment, remembering that this world is spiritual.

12

Boundaries

Why Boundaries Are Important

You have to think of boundaries as a protector. Your boundaries are rules that you would put in place to protect you and your peace. Many do not realize just how important boundaries are. Whether it is boundaries in a relationship or even with the people in your workplace. Those who have chosen to set strict boundaries have been set apart from the majority of people who will allow disrespect. For example, an individual could have a boundary in the workplace that demands their supervisor not call them after work hours without the overtime being reflected on their paycheck. It may sound shallow but having boundaries demands respect, it shows that you know your worth. Choosing to demand pay from a job that requires more of the time than you initially signed up for is the bare minimum. You have to know that your time is valuable. If you do not believe your time is valuable, why would anyone else? Many people will be offended by the boundaries you set and it shows their character in more ways than one. Those who respect you will respect your boundaries. Boundaries are important because they protect you. They can protect you from abuse, they can protect you from being overworked and underpaid, and they can protect your peace. The individual who tells their supervisor they will not work overtime without being paid is now treated as if they are worth it because they set a boundary.

Boundaries In Your Relationships

When discussing the topic of boundaries, many automatically think of relationships. This is because relationships are such a prominent topic, from romantic relationships to relationships with family and coworkers. Setting boundaries in a relationship will protect you, that is a fact. Many people choose not to set boundaries and unfortunately, choosing not to set boundaries is an indicator of a lack of self-love. Setting boundaries does not mean you don't show grace to other people, it means that you respect others but you also respect yourself and demand that same respect from others. We have to remember that different people come from different upbringings and this can affect how they treat others. Their treatment toward you is not always a reflection of you or your worth, but instead a reflection of them. Boundaries can be as simple as open and respectful communication.

Now, everyone does not have to like your boundaries, but if they are going to have a relationship with you then respecting your boundaries is the bare minimum. Please remember that the boundaries you have in place should not hurt others or disrespect their boundaries. Boundaries are to protect you and your peace. Another boundary one may have is to not be intimately touched on the first date or before truly getting to know someone. This is a boundary that should be discussed and respected. Once you disclose your boundaries to someone and they choose to ignore them, it is disrespectful to you. Anyone who values your time, attention, and energy will respect your boundaries.

The People-Pleaser

Let me start by saying, do not be afraid to take up space, you were created for a reason. With that being said, people-pleasing stems from childhood in most cases. Unfortunately, some were not taught to enforce boundaries or respect boundaries. Some grew up in homes where having boundaries was not allowed. Some were shamed or even punished for creating boundaries and made to believe that boundaries were not necessary. People-pleasers have a very high tendency to neglect their own needs by not setting boundaries. If you know you are a people-pleaser, it might be a great idea to figure out why. Another thing to do is to acknowledge who you are and the value you add to yourself and others. You cannot be afraid to demand the respect you deserve. Again, demanding respect and setting boundaries does not equate to rudeness or a lack of grace for others. In fact, to demand respect you must give respect. If you are respectful of others and also considerate of others, you should be treated with respect and consideration also. People-pleasers typically fail to set boundaries because they do not believe they are worthy of basic respect. Becoming the best version of yourself means that you love yourself enough to have boundaries.

Saying No

A big part of people-pleasing and setting boundaries is learning to say no. When you are not comfortable doing something or taking on a new task, saying no can prevent stress. I am not saying that you should not help others or tell people no each time they ask for help or request for you to do something. I am saying that you must have balance and if something genuinely does not feel good for your body then saying no is acceptable. Knowing when to say no is a matter of listening to your body and your intuition, it can save you from unnecessary stress. Many people may have the idea that telling someone no makes them a mean person, this is inaccurate. You must respect your own needs and value your feelings. Let's say someone invites you out somewhere and immediately you feel in your body that you do not want to go. Telling them yes when you in fact do not want to go is disrespecting yourself. You may feel guilty or responsible for their emotions but it is important to understand that you are not in control of others or their emotions. Learning to say no to certain plans sets you apart from the people who will just go with anything. It genuinely shows how much you respect yourself. Learning when to say no can protect you from people and situations that may ultimately make you uncomfortable. This is why boundaries and speaking up for yourself are so important.

13

The Path To Greatness

Your Path To Greatness

We have covered many topics in this book that will help you to become the version of you that God wants you to be. The topics discussed are not habits formed overnight most of the time. It is a journey, a journey that requires consistency and intentionality. You should always remember that you have a purpose and you should be actively working at your purpose. I will not tell you that it is easy or that you may not get tired. You have to remember that you are human and it may get overwhelming at times when working at your goals, especially when the results are not instantaneous. One thing for sure is that you will feel better overall when taking the necessary steps to reach your goals. This book allows you to do the inner work needed to access your goals. Many fail to realize that inner work is one of the most important parts of your journey. It is not just about becoming financially wealthy or obtaining your dream body. It is about overall mental, emotional, and spiritual well-being. You will unlock your potential in many different ways. Feeling better and more at peace will make it easier to continue on your journey. Again, you have to remember that your journey is about growth overall. Every day you should be doing something that is working toward a more fulfilling and peaceful life. This does not always include something that is physically or emotionally draining, this is sometimes a spa day or doing something that is relaxing. Becoming the best version of yourself is about knowing when to relax or when to work, this is what we have covered in this book. Enjoy this journey and thank The Most High for who He is and who He has called you to be. This is a blessing.

Believe

You have to have faith and believe in yourself. When you are striving to become who it is that you want to be, you must already believe that what it is you want is obtainable. The importance of believing that you can become the best version of yourself is more important than you may realize. Maybe you have been stuck in a place of anxiety or lack for so long that you do not feel as though it is obtainable, let me tell you that if you want it then it is obtainable. Today you must release all negative thoughts and thought patterns. Negative thinking can be a product of what you have gone through but it is time to release those old thinking patterns. Negative thinking is just that, negative. You should strive for positive thinking and peaceful thoughts. This is not to say that you will not have doubts at times. Again, you are human. However, when doubts come you should be replacing them with positive affirmations. Think, speak, and believe for the best. Things may not always go the way that you plan but trust in the process and trust God. Each time you state a positive affirmation, it should be met with faith and belief. If you are telling yourself that you will be great, you must believe it.

Permission To Be Great

One of the biggest reasons people doubt their potential is because no one around them has achieved the heights they aim to achieve. When you don't have people around you who have already done what it is you strive to do, it can cause you to question whether or not it is truly obtainable. One thing I can recommend is to study those who have done what it is you are working toward. From obtaining your dream body to starting the business you've desired for some time. Study those who have already done it, it will give you the permission you may subconsciously desire to jump into your desire. Decide today what it is you want and begin working at it.

14

Consistency Is Key

Everyone Wants The Best

Have you ever noticed how packed the crowds are when watching the replays of seminars on becoming better? Have you ever noticed the amount of people that engage in self-help content online? Or what about the overwhelming amount of social media posts at the beginning of the calendar year with resolutions people intend to follow to become the best version of themselves? This proves that a lot of people want to be better, they want to grow and become successful. Billions of dollars are spent yearly on self-help books, content, and coaching by those who desire to become better. This is great, but there is a big difference between the individuals who will grow versus the individuals who remain stagnant. The difference is consistency. The Bible tells us that we need faith but with that faith, we also have to have works. The work we put in must be met with consistency when trying to achieve certain goals.

Why You Need Consistency

Surely you have heard many say, "Consistency is key", but why is it a key? One reason I believe is because it separates the ones who genuinely want success versus the ones who are stagnant and content in their suffering. Another reason is due to the fact that in your journey to success, you will likely be met with opposition. When you are met with opposition and you give up, it shows God you may not exactly be ready for what you are asking for, it also shows you still have more growing and maturing to do. When you choose to combat opposition with consistency you are proving that you are ready for what it is you are asking for. Take a business owner for example. When someone chooses to start a business there are so many different things they must learn. If a new business owner cowers at the excess amount of research their new business requires, it shows they may not be able to handle running their own business. If you are someone who genuinely wants to be better you must practice consistency. Prove to The Creator of The Universe that you are determined and that you do want to be better.

Being Consistent

Being consistent not only proves you are serious to The Creator, but you are proving something to yourself. Every time you choose inconsistency you are showing to yourself that you cannot trust yourself. When you show yourself constant inconsistency, it will begin to dwindle at your self-confidence. Consistency in working on yourself is a sign of self-love because every time you are consistent in your level-up journey, your insecurities fade and your confidence grows. Confidence is obtained by working on yourself and also showing up for yourself. Of course, you want people to show up for you and treat you with the love, kindness, and respect you believe you deserve, so you must show up for yourself also.

Discipline

The truth is that motivation is a fleeting emotion. It's unfortunate because if the individuals who wanted to become better were motivated every day, they'd probably reach their goals a lot easier. This is why you need discipline. Yes, consistency sounds easy but in reality, there are days you might feel tired or overwhelmed and you may not want to work on yourself. When those moments come, you must rely on discipline. The way that we become disciplined is by repetition and forming good habits. Motivation is a feeling, a great one at that. Discipline is a choice, an action. Understanding the importance of discipline can be the start to achieving your goals. Now be mindful, discipline does not mean that you should ignore your body or your intuition. For example, there may be a day when you genuinely feel the need to skip the gym because your body is telling you it needs to rest. Choosing to listen to your body is a form of self-love. There are times when our bodies tell us not to eat something, not to go somewhere or not to be around certain people and we should listen. Make the choices necessary for your growth and aim to be consistent with them. Your choice to read a book that was written to help you become a better you is a great start. Now with the knowledge and wisdom you have received, let it be the commencement of your journey to becoming the best version of you.

Reminders and Motivation

What you do today matters, it sets the tone for the future.

Do not rely on the feeling of motivation to reach your goals of success, rely on consistency.

Love yourself the way you want others to love you. Treat yourself with the love and respect you want others to treat you with.

Don't be afraid to show up as you. People are craving your authenticity.

Get your boundaries and stick to them. You will repel people and situations that are not for you.

People usually know what it is you deserve, but if you don't know your worth then why would they give you all that is deserved? Know your worth.

You have all that you need to become the best version of yourself.

Gratitude in your current level is the prerequisite to your next level.

True success is when God is in it. Success without God is temporary.

Your value does not come from other people, it comes from God.

Confidence is built when you keep the promises you make to yourself.

Be patient with yourself.

Be consistent, work smart, and have gratitude.

Be kind to yourself.

Self-love is not the absence of love for others.

Connecting to The Most High is essential for your growth and success.

Surround yourself with people who want the best for you.

Be okay with walking away from situations that do not serve your highest good.

When you respect yourself. others will find it difficult to
disrespect you.

Affirmations, Just For You

Self-Love, Self-Concept, and Confidence Affirmations

I AM BLESSED.

I AM LOVED.

I AM SMART.

I AM STRONG.

I AM POWERFUL.

I AM KIND.

I AM GRATEFUL.

I AM APPRECIATIVE.

I RELEASE THE NEED FOR COMPARISON AND EMBRACE WHO I AM.

I AM ENOUGH.

I AM CONFIDENT.

I HONOR WHO I AM AND WHO GOD HAS CALLED ME TO BE.

I AM WORTHY OF LOVE AND RESPECT.

I RESPECT MYSELF.

I LOVE MYSELF.

I CARE FOR MYSELF.

I HONOR MY BODY.

I RESPECT MY NEEDS.

I SET CLEAR BOUNDARIES.

I DESERVE HAPPINESS.

I PRACTICE SELF-LOVE AND SELF-COMPASSION AND EXTEND THAT SAME LOVE AND COMPASSION TO OTHERS.

I AM CONFIDENT IN MY ABILITY TO ACHIEVE MY GOALS.

I BELIEVE IN MYSELF.

I EMBRACE MY TALENTS.

I AM LOVED AND WORTHY.

Prosperity and Abundance Affirmations

I ATTRACT GREAT OPPORTUNITIES.

I ATTRACT PEACE.

I ATTRACT LOVE.

I ATTRACT GOOD RELATIONSHIPS.

I ATTRACT HAPPINESS.

I AM A MAGNET FOR SUCCESS.

I AM A MAGNET FOR LOVE.

I RELEASE THE LIMITING BELIEFS THAT NO LONGER SERVE ME.

I ATTRACT PROSPEROUS OPPORTUNITIES THAT ALIGN WITH MY PURPOSE AND PASSION.

I RELEASE THE SCARCITY MINDSET AND ACCEPT THERE IS MORE THAN ENOUGH WEALTH TO GO AROUND.

Health and Well-Being Affirmations

I AM HEALTHY

I WILL NOURISH MY BODY.

I NOURISH MY MIND AND BODY.

I AM HEALTHY AND WHOLE.

I BALANCE WORK, RELAXATION, AND PLAY.

I LISTEN TO MY BODY AND WHAT MY BODY NEEDS.

I PRIORITIZE SELF-CARE.

I AM IN TUNE WITH MY BODY'S NEEDS AND I HONOR ITS SIGNAL FOR RELAXATION AND NOURISHMENT.

I RELEASE ANXIETY AND FEAR.

I WELCOME AND EMBRACE HEALTH AND VITALITY.

MY BODY IS A TEMPLE OF HEALTH AND VITALITY.

I AM DESERVING OF HEALTH AND JOY.

I RELEASE ANY TENSION AND STRESS.

I ATTRACT PEACE.

I AM GENTLE AND PATIENT WITH MYSELF.

I MAKE CHOICES THAT SUPPORT MY WELL-BEING.

MY MENTAL HEALTH IS A PRIORITY.

MY MIND THINKS PEACEFUL THOUGHTS.

HAPPINESS IS MY BIRTHRIGHT.

I RELEASE ALL WORRY AND FEAR.

I EMBRACE THE POWER OF A CALM MIND.

MY BODY IS HEALTHY AND STRONG.

I MAKE MINDFUL CHOICES THAT PROMOTE MY WELL-BEING.

I AM PROTECTED.

I AM HEALTHY, HAPPY, AND WHOLE.

I LISTEN TO MY BODY AND HONOR ITS NEED FOR SELF-CARE.

SELF-CARE IS A GIFT THAT I GIVE TO MYSELF.

I AM WILLING TO INVEST IN SELF-CARE.

I PRIORITIZE MY PEACE.

I HONOR MY WELL-BEING.

MY MIND IS FILLED WITH POSITIVE THOUGHTS.

Affirmations For Success

I ATTRACT SUCCESS AND PROSPERITY THROUGH MY EFFORTS.

I AM CAPABLE OF ACHIEVING MY GOALS.

I AM PERSISTENT IN THE PURSUIT OF MY GOALS.

EVERYTHING WORKS OUT FOR ME.

I AM WORTHY OF SUCCESS.

I SURROUND MYSELF WITH PEOPLE WHO SUPPORT MY GOALS.

I WILL ACHIEVE GREATNESS.

PROSPERITY FLOWS TO ME AND THROUGH ME.

I AM FULL OF POSITIVITY.

TODAY I RELEASE OLD HABITS THAT DO NOT SERVE THE BEST VERSION OF ME.

I AM CAPABLE OF ATTRACTING ABUNDANCE OF GREAT THINGS.

I BELIEVE IN MYSELF.

I LET GO OF NEGATIVE BELIEFS THAT ARE IN THE WAY OF MY SUCCESS.

EVERY DAY I BECOME MORE CONFIDENT AND SUCCESSFUL.

WEALTH CONSTANTLY FLOWS TO ME.

I AM COMMITTED TO ACHIEVING SUCCESS IN ALL AREAS OF LIFE.

I AM CONFIDENT IN MY SKILLS AND GIFTS.

I AM WORTHY OF INVESTING IN MYSELF.

I ATTRACT GREAT OPPORTUNITIES.

I ATTRACT GOOD RELATIONSHIPS.

I AM A MAGNET FOR POSITIVE PEOPLE.

I AM EXCITED TO WORK AT MY GOALS.

I AM THANKFUL FOR MY PURPOSE.

Psalm 91; A Psalm of King David

1 He that dwelleth in the secret place of The Most High shall abide under the shadow of The Almighty.

2 I will say of The Lord, He is my refuge and my fortress: my God; in Him will I trust.

3 Surely He shall deliver thee from the snare of the fowler, and from the noisome pestilence.

4 He shall cover thee with His feathers, and under His wings shalt thou trust: His truth shall be thy shield and buckler.

5 Thou shall not be afraid for the terror by night; nor for the arrow that flieth by day;

6 Nor for the pestilence that walketh in darkness; nor for the destruction that wasteth at noonday.

7 A thousand shall fall at thy side, and ten thousand at thy right hand; but it shall not come nigh thee.

8 Only with thine eyes shalt thou behold and see the reward of the wicked.

9 Because thou hast made The Lord, which is my refuge, even The Most High, thy habitation;

10 There shall no evil befall thee, neither shall any plague come nigh thy dwelling.

11 For He shall give His angels charge over thee, to keep thee in all thy ways.

12 They shall bear thee up in their hands, lest thou dash thy foot against a stone.

13 Thou shall tread upon the lion and adder: the young lion and the dragon shalt thou trample under feet.

14 Because he hath set his love upon me, therefore will I deliver him: I will set him on high, because he hath known my name.

15 He shall call upon me, and I will answer him: I will be with him in trouble; I will deliver him and honour him.

16 With long life will I satisfy him, and shew him My salvation.

Arissa August is an author, a speaker, and a life coach. Her journey toward life coaching began when she made it a priority to connect with God. After truly connecting with God she realized there was much work to be done and she knew there was an assignment God had given her. Arissa strives to positively impact the world by teaching women and men the importance of self-love. Focusing more on the community of women, Arissa creates lessons and motivational content to educate women on the topic of relationships and self-love. She encourages people to build a relationship with God as this is the start of greatness.